PECULIAR
GOINGS
ON

PECULIAR GOINGS ON

Dave Walker

CANTERBURY
PRESS
Norwich

© Dave Walker 2012

First published in 2012 by the Canterbury Press Norwich
Editorial office
3rd Floor, Invicta House,
108–114 Golden Lane,
London EC1Y 0TG

Canterbury Press is an imprint of Hymns Ancient & Modern
Ltd (a registered charity)
13A Hellesdon Park Road, Norwich,
Norfolk, NR6 5DR, UK

www.canterburypress.co.uk

British Library Cataloguing in Publication data

A catalogue record for this book is available
from the British Library

978 1 84825 236 3

Printed and bound in Great Britain by
CPI Group (UK) Ltd, Croydon

USEFUL INFORMATION

FOR READERS

THINGS YOU WILL NEED:

IDEAL POSTURES:

SUGGESTED READING TIMES:

STORAGE IDEAS:

OTHERS WHO MIGHT ALSO QUITE LIKE A COPY:

THE PERIODIC TABLE
of CHURCHGOERS

V VICAR								**CW** ∴ CHURCH WARDEN
C CURATE	**CM** □ CHOIR MASTER/MISTRESS					**SN** SIDESPERSON	**ST** STAUNCH TRADITIONALIST	**T** ∴ TREASURER
FL FLOWER LADY	**DM** ◇ DEPUTY CHOIR MASTER/MISTRESS					**BE** BELL RINGER	**DI** DETERMINED INNOVATOR	**PCC** ∴ MEMBER
RE READER	**AC** ACOLYTE	**YM** YOUNG MOTHER	**NC** NOISY CHILD	**NR** + NOVICE PREACHER	**SS** ° SUNDAY SCHOOL TEACHER	**CH** ° CHORISTER	**CR** ⊕ CHRISTIAN ROCK FAN	**IB** × INSENSITIVE BUSYBODY
SE SERVER	**TH** THURIFER	**SP** SINGLE PERSON	**PA** PARISH ADMINISTRATOR	**YW** * YOUTH WORKER	**EP** ENTHUSIASTIC PARTICIPANT	**MG** MUSIC GROUP MEMBER	**CI** • CONCISE INTERCESSOR	**OP** ! OVERSENSITIVE PERSON
CS COFFEE SERVER	**OR** ORGANIST	VISITORS (SEE BELOW)	**OV** OFFICE VOLUNTEER	**YV** YOUTH CLUB VOLUNTEER	**WV** ° WILLING VOLUNTEER	**NP** ⊗ NON-CHANTING PRIEST	**QF** QUIET FAMILY	**JI** — JADED INDIVIDUAL

HM HOLIDAY MAKER	**PI** PILGRIM	**WC** WEDDING COUPLE	**DO** UNDERCOVER DIOCESAN OFFICIAL	**PO** PROSPECTIVE INCUMBENT	**CC** CHURCH CRAWLER	**OH** TURNED UP BY ACCIDENT

KEY

- ° RARE METALS
- ⊕ HEAVY METALS
- ∴ NOBLE GASSES
- □ GOOD CONDUCTIVITY
- ◇ GOOD SEMICONDUCTIVITY
- − HIGH ELECTRONEGATIVITY
- × QUITE DENSE
- ⊗ LOW MASS
- + EXISTS UNDER PRESSURE
- ! HIGHLY REACTIVE
- • AS YET UNDISCOVERED
- * NOT YET FOUND IN A STABLE STATE

CHURCH

EXPLAINED USING TRANSPORT METAPHORS

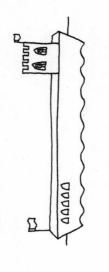

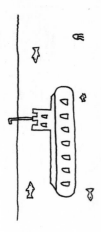

TAKES A LONG TIME TO CHANGE COURSE

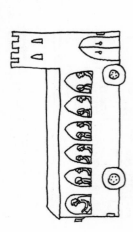

LOTS OF PASSENGERS

LOOKING OUT FOR OPPONENTS TO TORPEDO

STEERING BY ONE PERSON

THE SUNDAY MORNING SERVICE

TIMES AT WHICH IT CANNOT BE HELD

7 AM   8 AM   9 AM   10 AM   11 AM   12 MIDDAY

KEY

Z Z Z Z CAN'T GET EVERYONE
Z Z Z Z READY IN TIME

O O O O COINCIDES WITH
O O O O CHILDREN'S FOOTBALL

O O O O BREAKS UP THE
            DAY TOO MUCH

MORNING BELLS
ANNOY NEIGHBOURS

SHOPPERS WILL HAVE
TAKEN PARKING SPACES

CLASHES WITH GETTING
THE LUNCH ON

R R R WON'T ATTRACT THE
R R R YOUNGER GENERATION

MAKES MID-MORNING
COFFEE AWKWARD

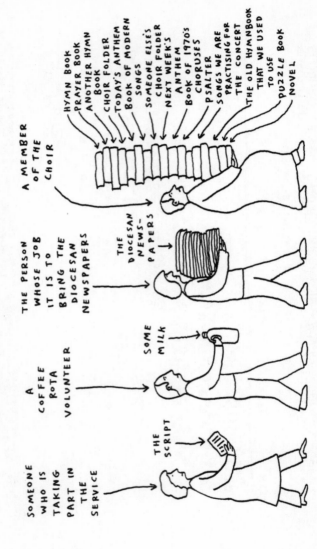

THINGS TO TAKE

ITEMS YOU WILL NEED IN CHURCH IF YOU ARE:

SOMEONE WHO IS TAKING PART IN THE SERVICE — THE SCRIPT

A COFFEE ROTA VOLUNTEER — SOME MILK

THE PERSON WHOSE JOB IT IS TO BRING THE DIOCESAN NEWSPAPERS — THE DIOCESAN NEWSPAPERS

A MEMBER OF THE CHOIR —
HYMN BOOK
PRAYER BOOK
ANOTHER HYMN BOOK
CHOIR FOLDER
TODAY'S ANTHEM
BOOK OF MODERN SONGS
SOMEONE ELSE'S CHOIR FOLDER
NEXT WEEK'S ANTHEM
BOOK OF 1970'S CHORUSES
PSALTER
SONGS WE ARE PRACTISING FOR THE CONCERT
THE OLD HYMNBOOK THAT WE USED TO USE
PUZZLE BOOK
NOVEL

CLOTHING

HOW TO DECIDE WHAT TO WEAR TO CHURCH SERVICES
DURING THE WINTER MONTHS

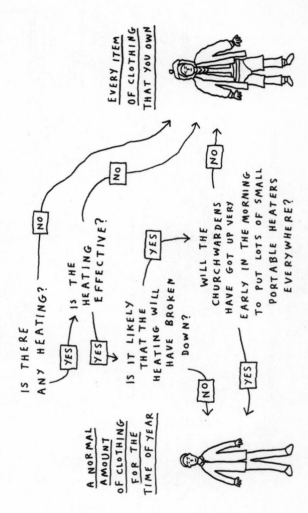

IS THERE
ANY HEATING?

YES — IS THE
HEATING
EFFECTIVE?

NO

YES

IS IT LIKELY
THAT THE
HEATING WILL
HAVE BROKEN
DOWN?

NO

YES

WILL THE
CHURCHWARDENS
HAVE GOT UP VERY
EARLY IN THE MORNING
TO PUT LOTS OF SMALL
PORTABLE HEATERS
EVERYWHERE?

NO

YES

A NORMAL
AMOUNT
OF CLOTHING
FOR THE
TIME OF YEAR

EVERY ITEM
OF CLOTHING
THAT YOU OWN

PARENTS

THINGS YOU WILL NEED TO TAKE TO CHURCH

VARIOUS SNACKS

A TOY THAT SQUEAKS

FELT TIP PENS

YOU CAN COLOUR THE BOOKS THAT ARE LEFT IN THE PEWS

POTTY / NAPPIES / PANTS

A BOUNCY BALL

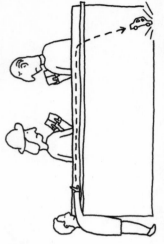

A CAR THAT DOES NOT QUITE FIT ON THE PEW LEDGE

PAPERWORK

YOU MAY NEED SOME OF THE FOLLOWING:

LARGE WAD OF PAPERWORK FROM SOME VERY IMPORTANT COMMITTEE OR OTHER

LARGE WAD OF RANDOM PAPERWORK TO MAKE IT LOOK AS IF YOU ARE ON SOME VERY IMPORTANT COMMITTEE OR OTHER

NOTEPAD AND PEN FOR "SERMON NOTES"

WORSHIPPING THROUGH THE MEDIUM OF DOODLING

RECEIPT FROM 1923 TO PROVE THAT THIS IS MY PEW

DIARY TO ORGANISE SOCIAL LIFE (PCC MEETINGS ETC)

THESE DAYS THEY CAN BE ELECTRONIC OWING TO TECHNOLOGY ETC

MOBILE TELEPHONES

WHY YOU SHOULD TAKE THEM TO CHURCH

WHY YOU SHOULD LEAVE THEM AT HOME

HEY... HAVE A LISTEN TO THIS — IT'S BRILLIANT

I'M IN CHURCH   I'M IN CHURCH
I'M IN CHURCH   I'M IN CHURCH
I'M IN CHURCH   I'M IN CHURCH
I'M IN CHURCH   I'M IN CHURCH
I'M IN CHURCH
I'M IN CHURCH   I'M IN CHURCH

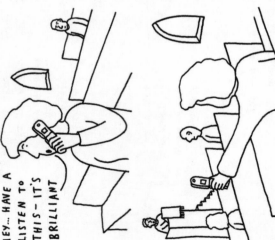

ARRIVING EARLY

HOW TO SPEND THE TIME BEFORE THE SERVICE

APPROPRIATE   BORDERLINE   INAPPROPRIATE

BUILDING A WALL
OF KNEELERS

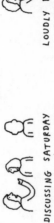

GETTING ALL OF THE HYMNS
READY IN SEPARATE BOOKS

SITTING
MOTIONLESS
WITH
REVERENT
EXPRESSION

DISCUSSING SATURDAY
EVENING'S ACTIVITIES

LOUDLY DISCUSSING SATURDAY
EVENING'S ACTIVITIES

TWEETING   CHIRPING

READING THE
NOTICE SHEET
QUIETLY AND
SENSIBLY

TRYING ON VESTMENTS
AND CHASING PEOPLE

EMERGENCY PROCEDURES

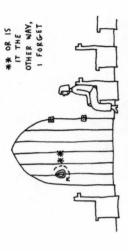

** OR IS
IT THE
OTHER WAY,
I FORGET

IF YOU ARE SEATED NEXT TO ONE OF THE DOORS
FAMILIARISE YOURSELF WITH ITS OPERATION

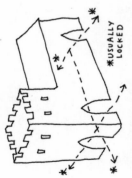

*USUALLY
LOCKED

KNOW WHERE THE EXITS ARE

PROCESS OUT IN AN ORDERLY FASHION

GET USED TO ADOPTING THE
BRACE POSITION

STANDING AND SITTING

WATCH TO SEE WHAT
OTHER PEOPLE ARE DOING

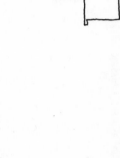

IF IN DOUBT ADOPT
A 'MID WAY' POSITION

SEE WHETHER IT SAYS ANYTHING
IN THE SERVICE BOOK

SIT
DOWN

LOOK OUT FOR SUBTLE HINTS
GIVEN BY THE CLERGY

THE HYMNS

HOW THEY ARE CHOSEN EVERY WEEK

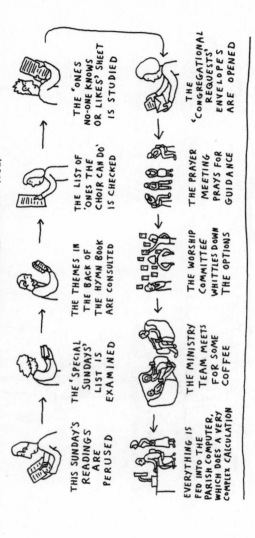

THIS SUNDAY'S READINGS ARE PERUSED

THE 'SPECIAL SUNDAYS' LIST IS EXAMINED

THE THEMES IN THE BACK OF THE HYMN BOOK ARE CONSULTED

THE LIST OF 'ONES THE CHOIR CAN DO' IS CHECKED

THE 'ONES NO-ONE KNOWS OR LIKES' SHEET IS STUDIED

EVERYTHING IS FED INTO THE PARISH COMPUTER, WHICH DOES A VERY COMPLEX CALCULATION

THE MINISTRY TEAM MEETS FOR SOME COFFEE

THE WORSHIP COMMITTEE WHITTLES DOWN THE OPTIONS

THE PRAYER MEETING PRAYS FOR GUIDANCE

THE 'CONGREGATIONAL REQUESTS' ENVELOPES ARE OPENED

MEANWHILE

THE MUSIC DIRECTOR JUST PICKS A FEW OF HER FAVOURITES

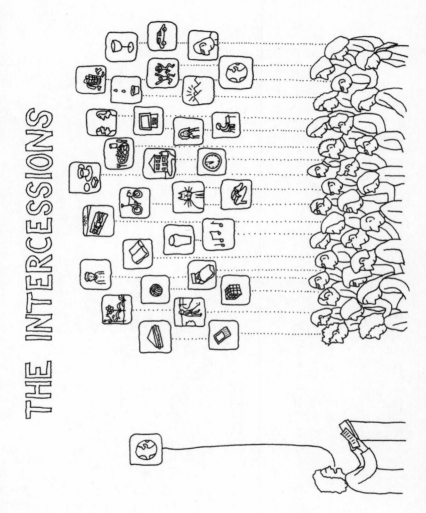

THE INTERCESSIONS

THE COLLECTION PLATE

YOUR OPTIONS AS IT APPROACHES

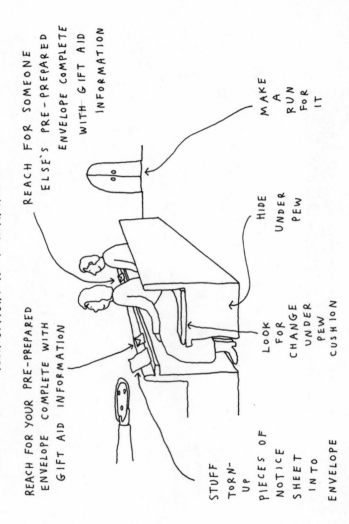

REACH FOR YOUR PRE-PREPARED
ENVELOPE COMPLETE WITH
GIFT AID INFORMATION

REACH FOR SOMEONE
ELSE'S PRE-PREPARED
ENVELOPE COMPLETE
WITH GIFT AID
INFORMATION

MAKE
A
RUN
FOR
IT

HIDE
UNDER
PEW

LOOK
FOR
CHANGE
UNDER
PEW
CUSHION

STUFF
TORN-
UP
PIECES OF
NOTICE
SHEET
INTO
ENVELOPE

COMMUNION
DOS AND DON'TS

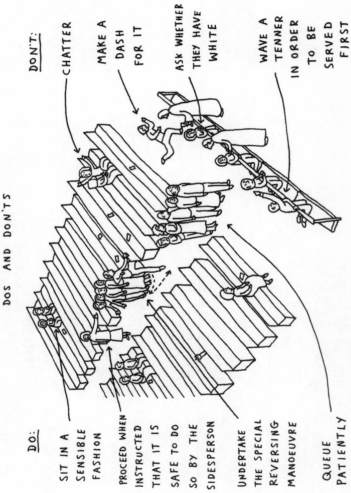

DO:

SIT IN A SENSIBLE FASHION

PROCEED WHEN INSTRUCTED THAT IT IS SAFE TO DO SO BY THE SIDESPERSON

UNDERTAKE THE SPECIAL REVERSING MANOEUVRE

QUEUE PATIENTLY

DON'T:

CHATTER

MAKE A DASH FOR IT

ASK WHETHER THEY HAVE WHITE

WAVE A TENNER IN ORDER TO BE SERVED FIRST

IRRITATING HABITS

SOME OF THE WORST HABITS ➡

WHY PEOPLE INDULGE IN THEM, ACCORDING TO OUR PANEL OF EXPERTS ➡

PEW KICKING

"THEY NEED TO USE THEIR FEET MORE. TRY PUTTING THEM IN THE PROCESSION"

WHISPERING AND CHATTERING

"THEY HAVE AN URGE TO SAY MORE. THE BEST WAY TO HELP THEM WOULD BE TO INCREASE THE LENGTH OF THE LITURGY"

COIN JINGLING

POCKET

"THEY WOULD LIKE TO GIVE MORE.

THIS COMPLAINT CAN OFTEN BE CURED USING A DIRECT DEBIT FORM"

UNGUARDED COUGHING/SNEEZING

"PROBABLY JUST FORGOT THEIR HANDKERCHIEF"

EXPLANATIONS

THINGS YOU WILL NEED TO EXPLAIN IF YOU BRING A FRIEND TO CHURCH

WHY THOSE PEOPLE ARE ACTING ODDLY

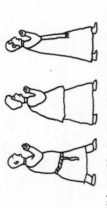

WHY THOSE PEOPLE ARE DRESSED STRANGELY

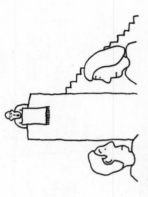

WHAT THAT MAN WAS TALKING ABOUT

WHY THOSE PEOPLE ARE LOOKING AT US IN A FUNNY WAY

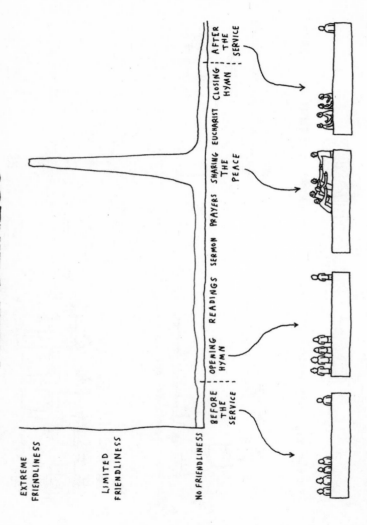

AT THE DOOR

HOW THE CLERGY REMEMBER ALL OF THE THINGS THAT PEOPLE TELL THEM

A
SPECIAL
NOTEBOOK →

PROBLEMS
COMPLAINTS
WOES
AILMENTS

THE PARISH
TYPIST

MEMORISING
USING A
MNEMONIC
(EXAMPLE) →

Mary
And
Deirdre

Only
Like
Dennis

Doing
Evensong
(Assorted
Reasons
Stated)

RADIO LINK
TO SECRET
CONTROL
CENTRE

KNOTS IN
HANDKERCHIEF →

CONSCIENTIOUS OBJECTORS

POSSIBLE ALTERNATIVE ARRANGEMENTS FOR THOSE WHO CANNOT,
IN ALL CONSCIENCE, RECEIVE THEIR AFTER-SERVICE REFRESHMENTS
FROM WHOEVER IT IS ON THE ROTA THIS WEEK

ONE COFFEE-TIME IN THE CHURCH HALL,
ANOTHER IN THE VESTRY

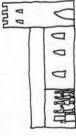

SEPARATE URNS WITHIN
THE SAME HALL

A SHARED URN, BUT
SEPARATE NOZZLES

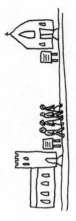

NO PROVISION - BUT YOU ARE WELCOME TO GET
YOUR COFFEE FROM THE CHURCH DOWN THE ROAD

THE HIERARCHY OF BISCUITS

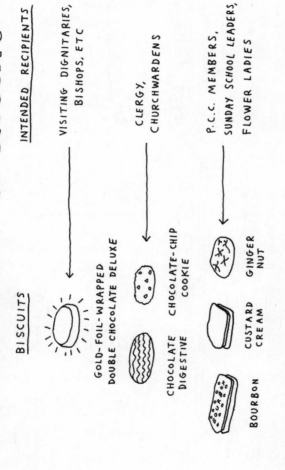

BISCUITS

INTENDED RECIPIENTS

VISITING DIGNITARIES, BISHOPS, ETC

GOLD-FOIL-WRAPPED DOUBLE CHOCOLATE DELUXE

CLERGY, CHURCHWARDENS

CHOCOLATE DIGESTIVE

CHOCOLATE-CHIP COOKIE

P.C.C. MEMBERS, SUNDAY SCHOOL LEADERS, FLOWER LADIES

BOURBON

CUSTARD CREAM

GINGER NUT

REGULAR CONGREGATION, CHILDREN, THE YOUTH WORKER

THOSE PINK WAFER ONES

'NICE' BISCUIT

MALTED MILK

RICH TEA

SIDESPERSONS

THE UNFORESEEN RESULTS OF ALIENATING THEM

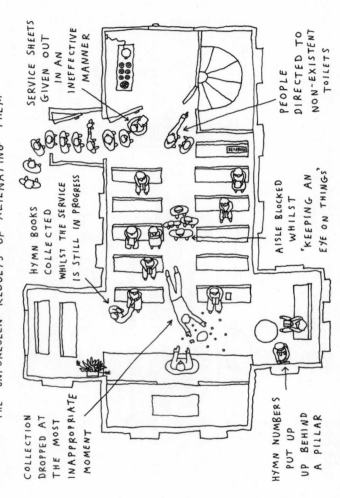

SERVICE SHEETS GIVEN OUT IN AN INEFFECTIVE MANNER

PEOPLE DIRECTED TO NON-EXISTENT TOILETS

HYMN BOOKS COLLECTED WHILST THE SERVICE IS STILL IN PROGRESS

AISLE BLOCKED WHILST "KEEPING AN EYE ON THINGS"

COLLECTION DROPPED AT THE MOST INAPPROPRIATE MOMENT

HYMN NUMBERS PUT UP UP BEHIND A PILLAR

THE BELL-RINGERS

HOW THEY GET IN AND OUT OF THE CHURCH BUILDING WITHOUT ANYONE ACTUALLY SEEING THEM

① A SKILFUL OPERATION INVOLVING AN AERIAL ASSAULT
② A CLEVER TACTIC INVOLVING A ROPE
③ A CUNNING PLOY INVOLVING A CAMP BED
④ A DEFT MANOEUVRE INVOLVING A FLOWER ARRANGEMENT
⑤ A CANNY STRATAGEM INVOLVING A SUBTERRANEAN PASSAGEWAY

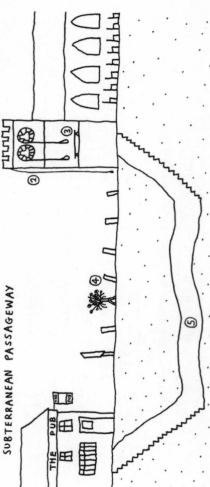

THE BELL-RINGERS

USEFUL INFORMATION FOR NEW RECRUITS

THINGS YOU WILL NEED

ROPE

BELL

THESE ARE USUALLY PROVIDED

BASIC INSTRUCTIONS

PULL THE ROPE WHEN DIRECTED

WHAT COULD BE SIMPLER?

SIGNIFICANT ACHIEVEMENTS ARE MARKED ON BOARDS ON THE WALLS OF THE TOWER

A QUARTER PEAL WAS RUNG HERE 14 JULY 1987

A FULL PEAL WAS RUNG HERE 20 FEB 2002

CONGRATULATIONS MARK ON PASSING YOUR DRIVING TEST BEST WISHES FROM US ALL

THIS IS THE MAN WHO RUINED A FULL PEAL WHEN HE ANSWERED HIS MOBILE TELEPHONE. THE OTHER RINGERS ARE NOT TERRIBLY HAPPY WITH HIM

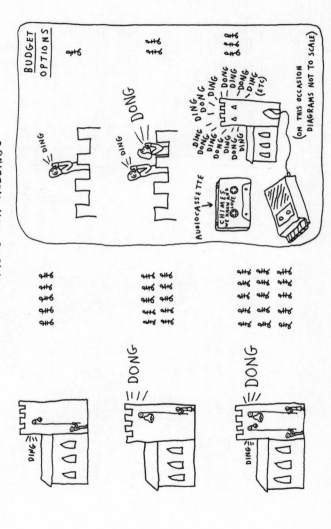

THE BELLS

SCALE OF CHARGES FOR WEDDINGS

THE PARISH OFFICE

ADVICE FOR VOLUNTEERS

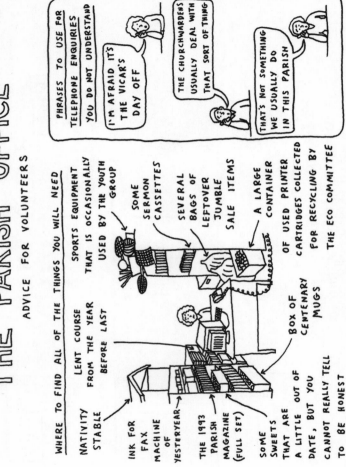

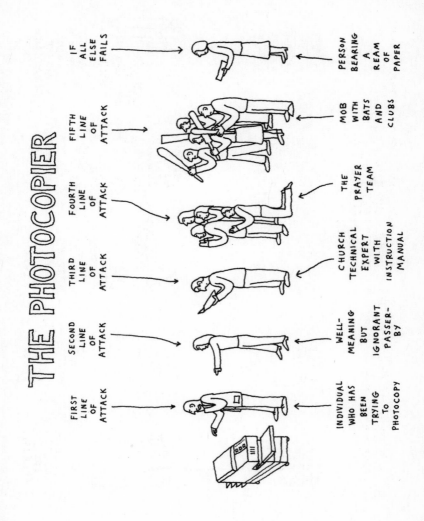

THE PHOTOCOPIER

FIRST LINE OF ATTACK

SECOND LINE OF ATTACK

THIRD LINE OF ATTACK

FOURTH LINE OF ATTACK

FIFTH LINE OF ATTACK

IF ALL ELSE FAILS

INDIVIDUAL WHO HAS BEEN TRYING TO PHOTOCOPY

WELL-MEANING BUT IGNORANT PASSER-BY

CHURCH TECHNICAL EXPERT WITH INSTRUCTION MANUAL

THE PRAYER TEAM

MOB WITH BATS AND CLUBS

PERSON BEARING A REAM OF PAPER

THE CHURCH NOTICE SHEET

MARKING THE ANNIVERSARIES

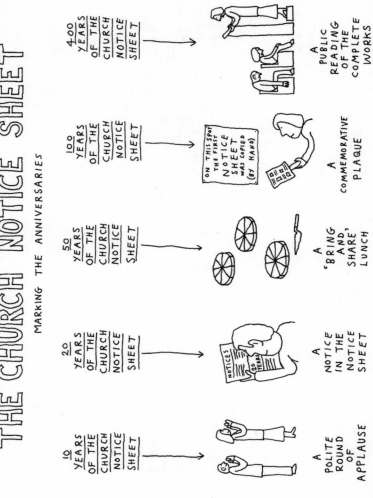

SPRING CLEANING

SORTING THROUGH THE CONTENTS OF THE CHURCH OFFICE CUPBOARD

ACETATES

THINGS THAT CAN BE DONE WITH DISUSED BATCHES

COLLATE THEM INTO ONE GIANT
TRANSPARENT HYMN BOOK

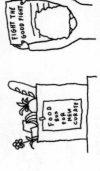

UTILISE THEM WHEN DECORATING
THE CURATE'S HOUSE

USE THEM TO REPAIR
THE CHURCH GUTTERING

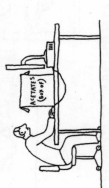

STORE THEM IN CASE ONPS COME BACK
INTO FASHION. THE CHURCH OFFICE
WOULD BE AN IDEAL PLACE FOR THIS

CHURCH CLEANING

THE PERILS OF OVER-ZEALOUSNESS

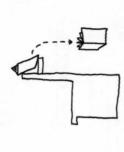

SLIDING HYMNBOOKS

AN UNSECURED ORGANIST

DAZZLING BRASSWORK

SLIPPERY COLLECTION PLATES

HASSOCKS

WHAT HAPPENS TO THEM DURING THE WEEK?

SOME ARE LENT OUT

KNEELER LENDING LIBRARY

A FEW ARE PILFERED
(VERY TRICKY TO DETECT)

PENITENT KNEELER
THIEF RETURNS STASH,
HAVING BEEN
CONVERTED BY
EMBROIDERED MESSAGES

THE CLERGY USE THE REMAINDER FOR TEAM-BUILDING EXERCISES

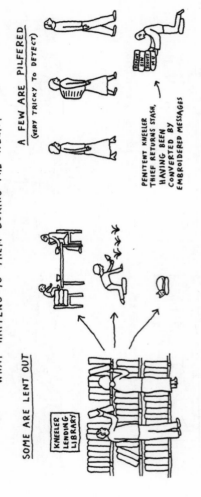
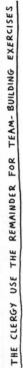
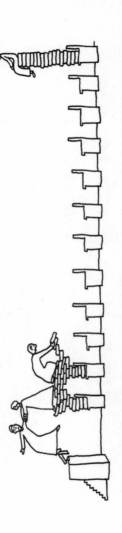

LONG SERVING PARISHIONERS

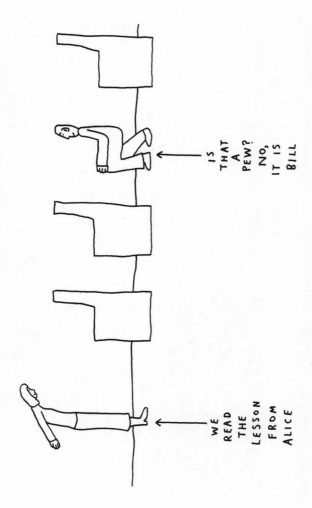

WE
READ
THE
LESSON
FROM
ALICE

IS
THAT
A
PEW?
NO,
IT IS
BILL

DIAGRAM SHOWING HOW THEY BECAME PART OF THE CHURCH FURNITURE

MECHANISATION

MODERN INNOVATIONS THAT ARE KILLING OFF THE TRADITIONAL CHURCH VOLUNTEER

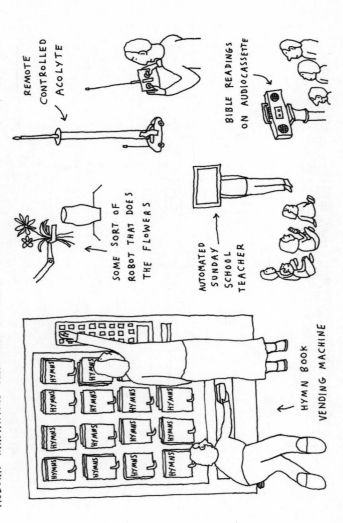

REMOTE CONTROLLED ACOLYTE

BIBLE READINGS ON AUDIOCASSETTE

SOME SORT OF ROBOT THAT DOES THE FLOWERS

AUTOMATED SUNDAY SCHOOL TEACHER

HYMN BOOK VENDING MACHINE

THE CHURCH EXTENSION

THE PLANS, DRAWN UP AFTER CONSULTATION WITH ALL INTERESTED PARTIES

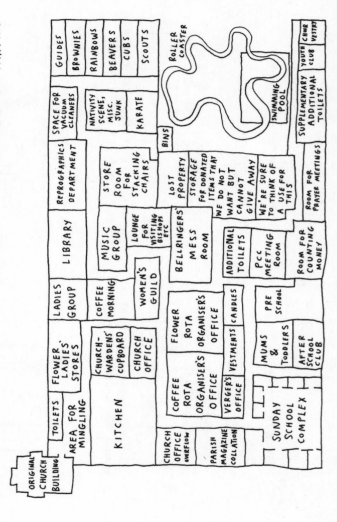

POLITICS

EVENTS OBSERVED FOLLOWING THE CHURCH COUNCIL ELECTIONS

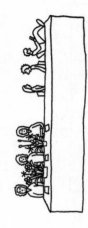

A COALITION BETWEEN THE FLOWER LADIES AND THE YOUTH GROUP

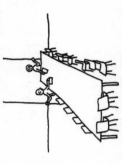

THE BELL RINGERS ATTEMPTING TO FORM A MINORITY PCC

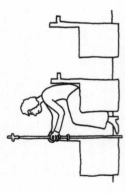

THE OUTGOING CHURCHWARDEN STILL OCCUPYING THE CHURCHWARDEN'S PEW

THE RECTOR BEING GIVEN A MANDATE TO RULE (I DID NOT KNOW WHAT A MANDATE LOOKED LIKE, SO I HAVE DRAWN A PINEAPPLE)

THE NEW P.C.C.

HOW THE RESPONSIBILITIES ARE DIVIDED UP

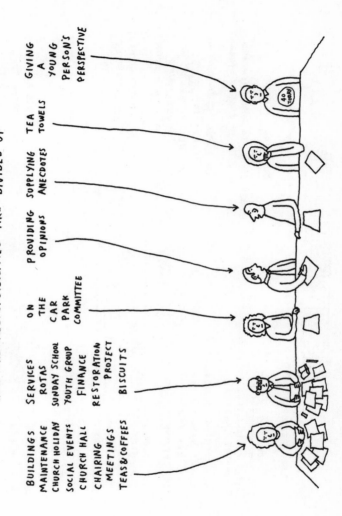

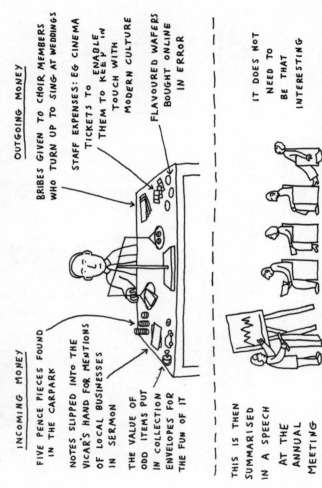

THE TREASURER

THE TREASURER'S JOB IS TO COUNT THE INCOMING AND OUTGOING MONEY

INCOMING MONEY

FIVE PENCE PIECES FOUND IN THE CARPARK

NOTES SLIPPED INTO THE VICAR'S HAND FOR MENTIONS OF LOCAL BUSINESSES IN SERMON

THE VALUE OF ODD ITEMS PUT IN COLLECTION ENVELOPES FOR THE FUN OF IT

OUTGOING MONEY

BRIBES GIVEN TO CHOIR MEMBERS WHO TURN UP TO SING AT WEDDINGS

STAFF EXPENSES: EG CINEMA TICKETS TO ENABLE THEM TO KEEP IN TOUCH WITH MODERN CULTURE

FLAVOURED WAFERS BOUGHT ONLINE IN ERROR

THIS IS THEN SUMMARISED IN A SPEECH AT THE ANNUAL MEETING

IT DOES NOT NEED TO BE THAT INTERESTING

THE CHURCH BUDGET

WHERE THE AXE IS LIKELY TO FALL

SERMONS
6 MINUTES SHORTER

PRINTING
ONLY INTERESTING NOTICES ALLOWED

NOTICES

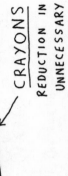

LILAC
TURQUOISE
PUCE

CRAYONS
REDUCTION IN UNNECESSARY COLOURS

WASTE
CUTTING DOWN ON IT

IDEAS

FOR THE FUTURE DIRECTION OF THE PARISH

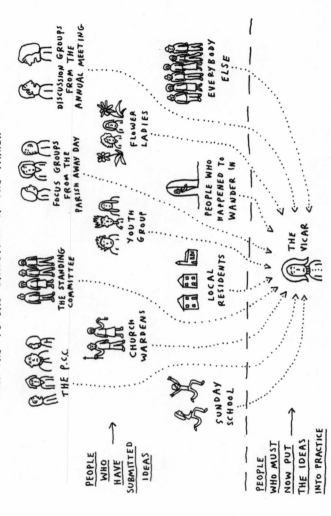

PEOPLE WHO HAVE SUBMITTED IDEAS →

THE P.C.C.

CHURCH WARDENS

THE STANDING COMMITTEE

YOUTH GROUP

FOCUS GROUPS FROM THE PARISH AWAY DAY

FLOWER LADIES

DISCUSSION GROUPS FROM THE ANNUAL MEETING

EVERYBODY ELSE

SUNDAY SCHOOL

LOCAL RESIDENTS

PEOPLE WHO HAPPENED TO WANDER IN

THE VICAR

PEOPLE WHO MUST NOW PUT → THE IDEAS INTO PRACTICE

LITURGICAL DANCE

HOW TO NIP IT IN THE BUD

ANTI-DANCE PAINT

TREAT THE
AFFECTED REGION

BUY UP ENTIRE LOCAL STOCKS
OF FLAGS AND RIBBONS

←-POTENTIAL DANCING-→
SPACE

INSTALL EXTRA PEWS IN THE
THREATENED AREA

DIRGES
WE KNOW
AND LOVE

VOL I

ERADICATE RHYTHM
FROM ALL HYMNS

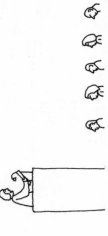

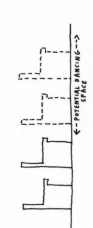

INCREASE SERMON LENGTH SO THAT THERE
IS NO TIME FOR THAT KIND OF THING

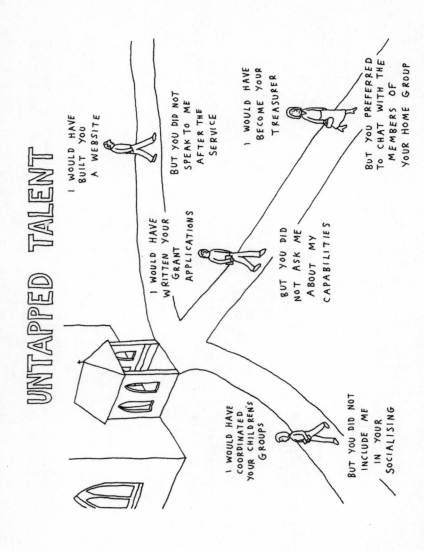

THE AREA DEAN'S VISIT

A RARE SIGHTING OF THE CONFIDENTIAL CHECKLIST

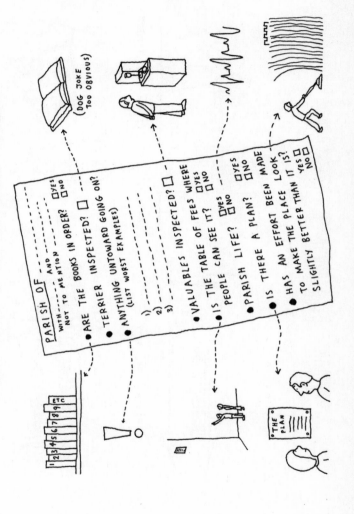

(DOG JOKE TOO OBVIOUS)

PARISH OF _____ AND _____
WITH _____ NOT TO MENTION _____

- ARE THE BOOKS IN ORDER? ☐ ☐YES ☐NO
- TERRIER INSPECTED? ☐
- ANYTHING UNTOWARD GOING ON?
  (LIST WORST EXAMPLES)
  1) _____
  2) _____
  3) _____
- VALUABLES INSPECTED? ☐
- IS THE TABLE OF FEES WHERE PEOPLE CAN SEE IT? ☐YES ☐NO
- PARISH LIFE? ☐YES ☐NO
- IS THERE A PLAN? ☐YES ☐NO
- HAS AN EFFORT BEEN MADE TO MAKE THE PLACE LOOK BETTER THAN IT IS? ☐YES ☐NO

1 2 3 4 5 6 7 8 9 ETC

THE PLAN

THE BISHOP'S VISIT

THINGS THAT MUST BE DONE

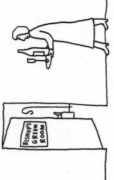

PREPARING THE WAY

CATERING FOR SPECIAL REQUIREMENTS

KEEPING UNDESIRABLE ELEMENTS
AT A SAFE DISTANCE

WRITING IN THE BOOKS TO MAKE IT LOOK
AS IF THERE ARE REGULAR SERVICES

THE BRING AND SHARE LUNCH

SUCCESSFUL STRATEGIES FOR RICH PICKINGS

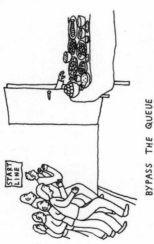

BYPASS THE QUEUE

VOLUNTEER TO HELP

DISTRACT THE COMPETITION

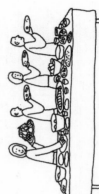

GO LAST

(NOTE: RISKY. RELIES ON THE ABSTEMIOUSNESS OF OTHERS)

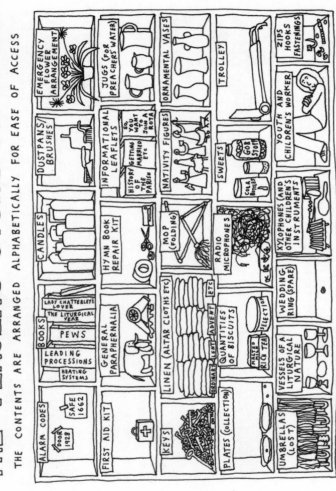

THE VERGER'S STORE CUPBOARD

THE CONTENTS ARE ARRANGED ALPHABETICALLY FOR EASE OF ACCESS

THE LADDERS IN THE NORTH TRANSEPT

WHAT IS BEHIND THEM?

POSSIBILITIES

CREEPY CRAWLIES

THE LOST VESTRY KEY

ANCIENT GROTESQUES

FORMER CHURCHWARDENS

THAT ELUSIVE SERMON IDEA

A HIDDEN DOOR INTO A SECRET WORLD

LIGHT SWITCHES

A TYPICAL ARRANGEMENT

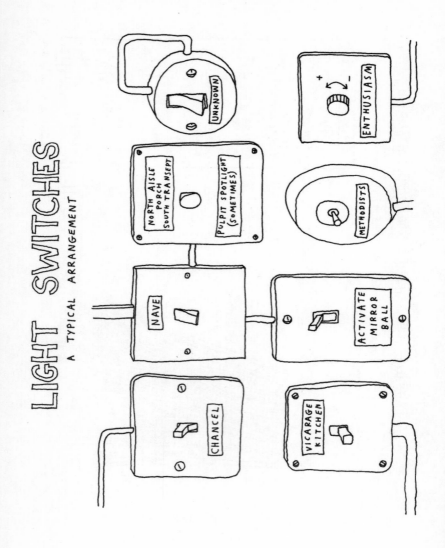

THE KEYS

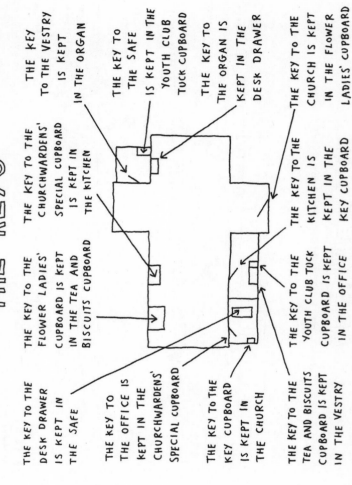

THE KEY TO THE DESK DRAWER IS KEPT IN THE SAFE

THE KEY TO THE FLOWER LADIES' CUPBOARD IS KEPT IN THE TEA AND BISCUITS CUPBOARD

THE KEY TO THE CHURCHWARDENS' SPECIAL CUPBOARD IS KEPT IN THE KITCHEN

THE KEY TO THE VESTRY IS KEPT IN THE ORGAN

THE KEY TO THE SAFE IS KEPT IN THE YOUTH CLUB TUCK CUPBOARD

THE KEY TO THE ORGAN IS KEPT IN THE DESK DRAWER

THE KEY TO THE OFFICE IS KEPT IN THE CHURCHWARDENS' SPECIAL CUPBOARD

THE KEY TO THE KEY CUPBOARD IS KEPT IN THE CHURCH

THE KEY TO THE YOUTH CLUB TUCK CUPBOARD IS KEPT IN THE OFFICE

THE KEY TO THE KITCHEN IS KEPT IN THE KEY CUPBOARD

THE KEY TO THE CHURCH IS KEPT IN THE FLOWER LADIES' CUPBOARD

THE KEY TO THE TEA AND BISCUITS CUPBOARD IS KEPT IN THE VESTRY

ARCHAEOLOGY

WHAT WE FOUND WHEN WE DUG DOWN

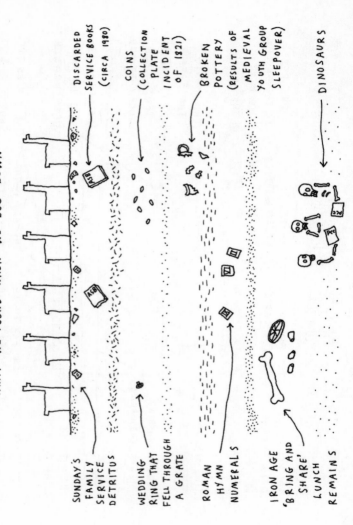

SUNDAY'S FAMILY SERVICE DETRITUS

DISCARDED SERVICE BOOKS (CIRCA 1980)

COINS (COLLECTION PLATE INCIDENT OF 1821)

WEDDING RING THAT FELL THROUGH A GRATE

BROKEN POTTERY (RESULTS OF MEDIEVAL YOUTH GROUP SLEEPOVER)

ROMAN HYMN NUMERALS

IRON AGE 'BRING AND SHARE' LUNCH REMAINS

DINOSAURS

THE CHURCH CAR PARK

HOW TO DEFEND IT FROM NON-CHURCHGOERS

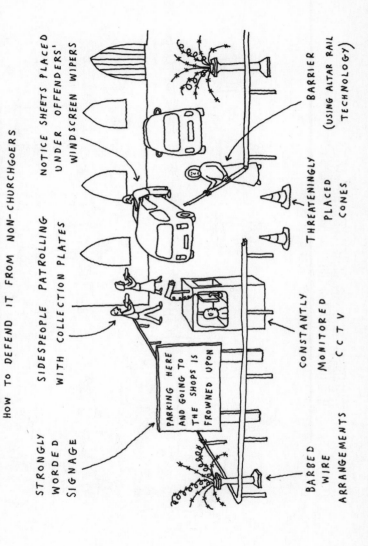

STRONGLY WORDED SIGNAGE

SIDESPEOPLE PATROLLING WITH COLLECTION PLATES

NOTICE SHEETS PLACED UNDER OFFENDERS' WINDSCREEN WIPERS

BARRIER (USING ALTAR RAIL TECHNOLOGY)

THREATENINGLY PLACED CONES

CONSTANTLY MONITORED CCTV

BARBED WIRE ARRANGEMENTS

PARKING HERE AND GOING TO THE SHOPS IS FROWNED UPON

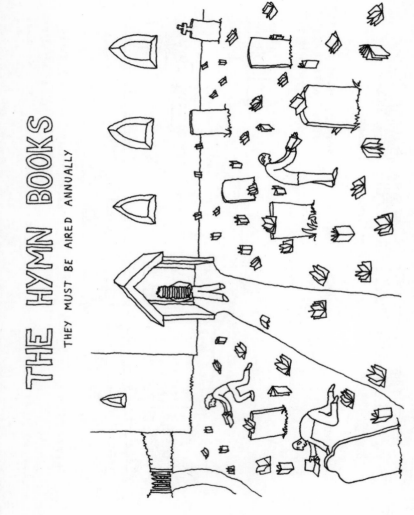

THE HYMN BOOKS

THEY MUST BE AIRED ANNUALLY

THE PIANO

HOW TO MOVE IT SLIGHTLY CLOSER TO THE LECTERN WITHOUT OBTAINING A FACULTY

WEEK 1

WEEK 2

WEEK 3

WEEK 4

WEEK 5

WEEK 6

WEEK 7

WEEK 8

THE SCHOOL HALL

THIS CONGREGATION MEETS FOR WORSHIP IN A SCHOOL HALL. NOT HAVING TO
MAINTAIN THEIR OWN BUILDING MAKES THEIR LIVES MUCH EASIER

ALTHOUGH THEY DO NEED
TO CARRY IN THEIR
OWN KEYBOARD

AND
FONT

AND
P.A.
SYSTEM

AND
DRUMS

AND
LECTERN

AND
ORGAN

AND
COFFEE
URN

CAR
PARK
9am

AND
PULPIT

AND
PEWS

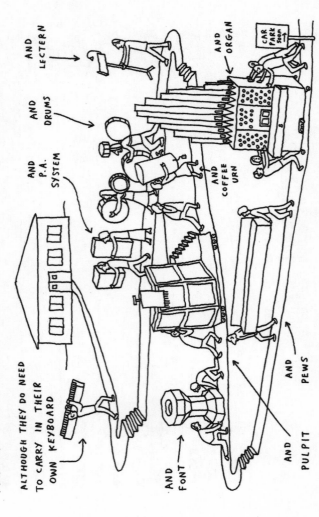

THE SUNDAY SCHOOL

WHAT THE LESSON PLAN SAYS:	WHAT THE LESSON PLAN MEANS:
EXPLORE THE TOPIC BY MEANS OF CREATIVE MEDIA	DO SOME COLOURING
ANALYSE THE THEME THROUGH A VARIETY OF PARTICIPATORY ACTIVITIES	DO SOME CUTTING AND STICKING
SPEND A FEW MOMENTS IN STILLNESS AND CONTEMPLATION MEDITATING ON THE SUBJECT	TRY TO GET EVERYONE TO SIT DOWN AND SHUT UP

THE SUNDAY SCHOOL

THIS MONTH'S CURRICULUM

BIBLE → STORY

CROSSING THE RED SEA

DANIEL IN THE LIONS' DEN

THE DAY OF PENTECOST

PAUL'S THIRD MISSIONARY JOURNEY

MAIN → LESSONS

BE NICE TO PEOPLE

TIDY YOUR BEDROOM

BE NICE TO PEOPLE

TIDY YOUR BEDROOM

BE NICE TO PEOPLE

TIDY YOUR BEDROOM

BE NICE TO PEOPLE

TIDY YOUR BEDROOM

THE SUNDAY SCHOOL

PROJECTS THAT PROVED, IN HINDSIGHT, TO BE RATHER OVERAMBITIOUS
GIVEN THE HOUR-LONG DURATION OF THE MORNING SERVICE

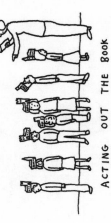

ACTING OUT THE BOOK
OF REVELATION

PERFECTING TALLIS'S
'SPEM IN ALIUM'

A LIFESIZE RECONSTRUCTION
OF NOAH'S ARK

LEARNING PSALM 119
OFF BY HEART

THE HOLIDAY CLUB

SIGNS THAT THERE HAS BEEN ONE TAKING PLACE DURING THE WEEK

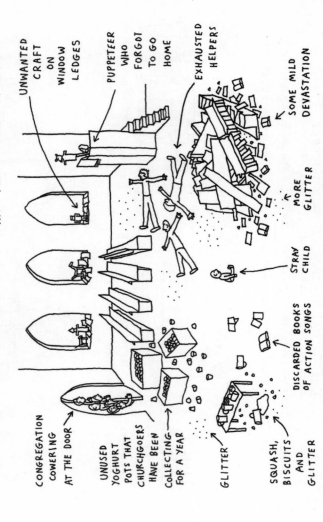

UNWANTED CRAFT ON WINDOW LEDGES

PUPPETEER WHO FORGOT TO GO HOME

EXHAUSTED HELPERS

SOME MILD DEVASTATION

MORE GLITTER

STRAY CHILD

CONGREGATION COWERING AT THE DOOR

UNUSED YOGHURT POTS THAT CHURCHGOERS HAVE BEEN COLLECTING FOR A YEAR

GLITTER

DISCARDED BOOKS OF ACTION SONGS

SQUASH, BISCUITS AND GLITTER

SCHOOL ASSEMBLIES

ADVICE FOR CLERGY

BE INTERESTING IF AT ALL POSSIBLE

MAKE SURE THAT YOUR MATERIAL
IS SUITABLE FOR THE AGE GROUP

DO NOT TRY TO ACT YOUNG
AND/OR COOL

DON'T GET THE KIDS TOO HYPED-UP

RUNNING A YOUTH CLUB

SO THAT THE SEVEN DEADLY SINS ARE NOT COMMITTED TOO OFTEN

GREED

HOGGING THE
TABLE TENNIS
TABLE SEVERELY
FROWNED UPON

VANITY

NO MIRRORS
AT CONVENIENT
HEIGHTS

LUST

SEPARATE ROOMS
FOR BOYS
AND GIRLS

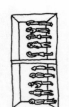

GLUTTONY

MAXIMUM
TUCK SHOP
SPEND OF
3 PENNY SWEETS

ENVY

ALL EXPENSIVE
GAMES CONSOLES
REPLACED WITH
BOARD GAMES

ANGER

SOOTHING
MUSIC PLAYED
THROUGH
LOUDSPEAKERS

SLOTH

NO CHAIRS

THE YOUTH GROUP

SIGNS OF INADEQUATE SUPERVISION

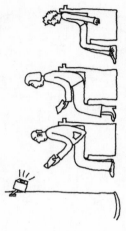

THE PA SYSTEM HAS BEEN TUNED
TO AN UNFAMILIAR RADIO STATION

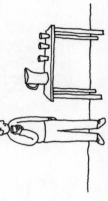

THE POST-SERVICE ORANGE SQUASH HAS
BEEN MADE AT NORMAL DILUTION

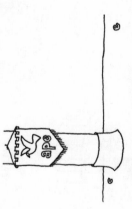

LETTERS ON BANNERS
HAVE BEEN REARRANGED

A PAGE HAS BEEN TURNED
IN THE LECTIONARY

THE ORDINATION RETREAT

WHAT HAPPENS ON IT?

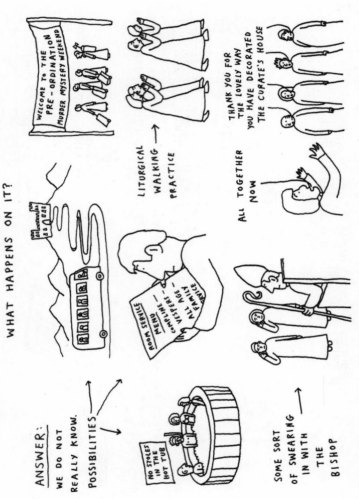

CURATES

HOW USEFUL ARE THEY?

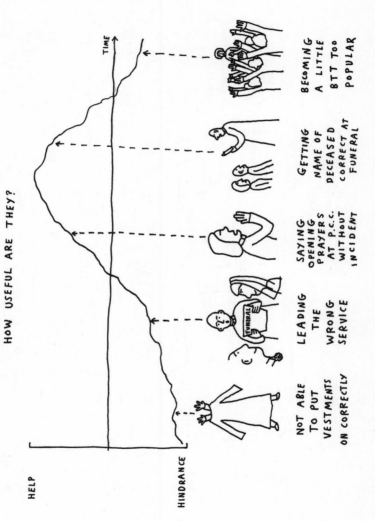

HELP

HINDRANCE

TIME

NOT ABLE TO PUT VESTMENTS ON CORRECTLY

LEADING THE WRONG SERVICE

SAYING OPENING PRAYERS AT P.C.C. WITHOUT INCIDENT

GETTING NAME OF DECEASED CORRECT AT FUNERAL

BECOMING A LITTLE BIT TOO POPULAR

WRITING A SERMON

THE PROCESS (SIMPLIFIED)

THE CLERGY SURPLUS STORES

EXCESS VESTMENTS ARE MADE AVAILABLE TO THE PUBLIC AT SPECIAL PRICES

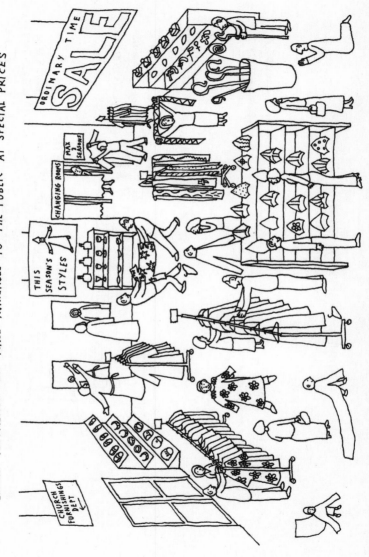

THE VICARAGE

WHAT IT IS USED FOR

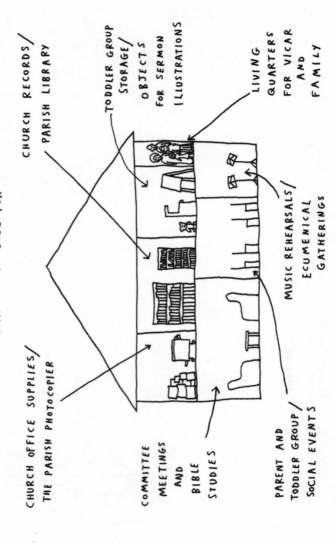

CHURCH RECORDS / PARISH LIBRARY

TODDLER GROUP STORAGE / OBJECTS FOR SERMON ILLUSTRATIONS

LIVING QUARTERS FOR VICAR AND FAMILY

CHURCH OFFICE SUPPLIES / THE PARISH PHOTOCOPIER

COMMITTEE MEETINGS AND BIBLE STUDIES

MUSIC REHEARSALS / ECUMENICAL GATHERINGS

PARENT AND TODDLER GROUP / SOCIAL EVENTS

AT THE VICARAGE

PEOPLE YOU MIGHT ENCOUNTER

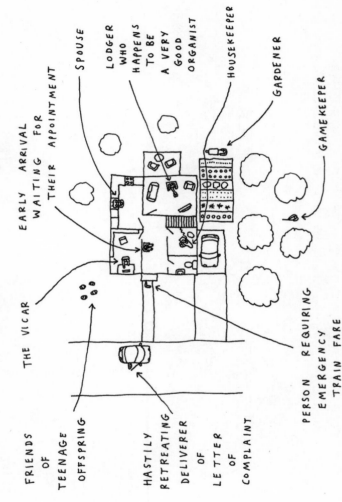

THE VICAR

EARLY ARRIVAL WAITING FOR THEIR APPOINTMENT

SPOUSE

LODGER WHO HAPPENS TO BE A VERY GOOD ORGANIST

HOUSEKEEPER

GARDENER

GAMEKEEPER

FRIENDS OF TEENAGE OFFSPRING

HASTILY RETREATING DELIVERER OF LETTER OF COMPLAINT

PERSON REQUIRING EMERGENCY TRAIN FARE

THE VICARAGE GARDEN

WHAT IT TELLS US

THE VICAR HAS BEEN NEGLECTING THE PARISH

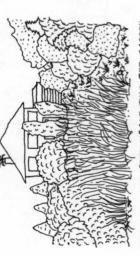

THE VICAR HAS BEEN NEGLECTING THE GARDEN

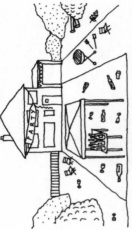

A PARTY HAS BEEN ENJOYED

A WORK PARTY IS BEING ENDURED

SUMMER FESTIVALS

SIGNS THAT CONGREGATION MEMBERS HAVE BEEN ATTENDING ONE

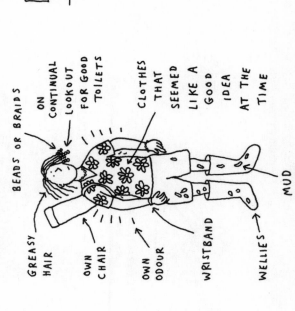

BEADS OR BRAIDS

ON CONTINUAL LOOKOUT FOR GOOD TOILETS

CLOTHES THAT SEEMED LIKE A GOOD IDEA AT THE TIME

GREASY HAIR

OWN CHAIR

OWN ODOUR

WRISTBAND

WELLIES

MUD

AFTER-SERVICE COFFEE

JOINING A QUEUE WHENEVER THEY SEE ONE

DURING HYMNS, THEY GOOD-NATUREDLY PUSH OR SLAM INTO OTHER PEOPLE FOR THE PURPOSES OF ENTERTAINMENT*

*MOSHING

GOING ON A RETREAT

THINGS YOU WILL PROBABLY DO

WRITE ON 'THE TIME THAT CHURCH HURT MY FEELINGS'

HOLD A PEBBLE

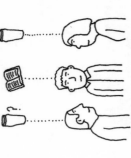

TRY TO WORK OUT WHICH OF THE OTHER PARTICIPANTS WOULD ALSO SECRETLY LIKE A TRIP TO THE PUB

UNDERTAKE DEVOTIONAL READING

HAVE MEALS IN SILENCE

THE HOLIDAY CAMP

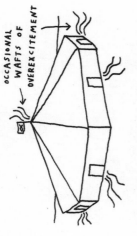

THE HOLIDAY CAMP FOR ENTHUSIASTIC
CHRISTIANS IS ABOUT TO BEGIN

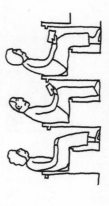

OCCASIONAL WAFTS of
OVEREXCITEMENT

NO ONE IS QUITE SURE WHAT GOES
ON INSIDE THE GIGANTIC TENT

NOTE
THAT
IT IS
FLAT

EARTH

ONE SUSPECTS THAT OUTLANDISH
THEORIES ARE BEING PROPOGATED

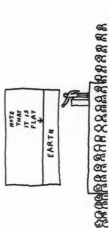

OUR ADVICE TO CHURCHGOERS: REMAIN WITHIN
THE SAFETY OF YOUR OWN CONGREGATION

THE CHRISTIAN CONFERENCE

A TYPICAL SCENE

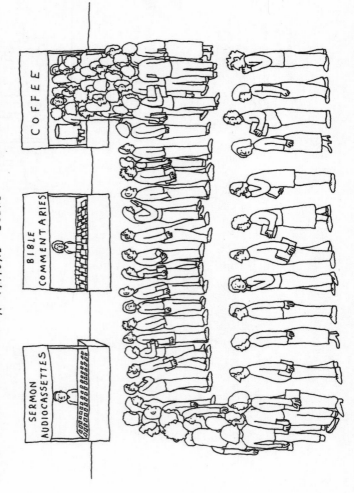

SERMON AUDIOCASSETTES

BIBLE COMMENTARIES

COFFEE

THE SEVEN WONDERS
OF THE DEANERY

① THE PYRAMIDAL HYMN BOOK STACK AT ST GEORGE'S

② THE LEANING TOMB STONE OF ST PETER'S

③ THE REASONABLY TIDY VESTRY AT EMMANUEL

④ THE PARTIALLY-LIT NORTH FACE OF ST ANDREW'S

⑤ THE IMPRESSIVE (SOME SAY COLOSSAL) PULPIT OF ST JOSEPH'S

⑥ THE HANGING VESTMENTS OF ST BARNABAS'

⑦ THE STATUE COMMEMORATING THE TIME BISHOP RHYS VISITED ST OLAVES

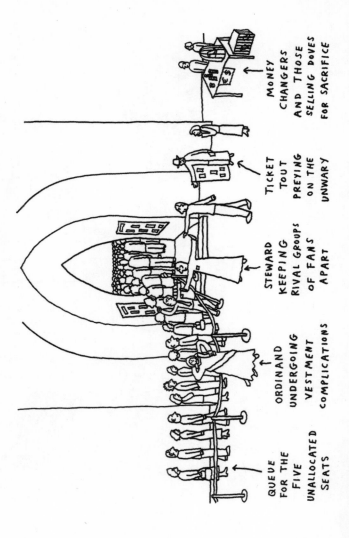

OUTSIDE THE CATHEDRAL

BEFORE THE ORDINATION SERVICE

QUEUE FOR THE FIVE UNALLOCATED SEATS

ORDINAND UNDERGOING VESTMENT COMPLICATIONS

STEWARD KEEPING RIVAL GROUPS OF FANS APART

TICKET TOUT PREYING ON THE UNWARY

MONEY CHANGERS AND THOSE SELLING DOVES FOR SACRIFICE

PEOPLE IN CASSOCKS

THEY WANDER AROUND IN THE CATHEDRAL, BUT UNTIL NOW NO ONE HAS KNOWN THE NATURE OF THEIR ERRANDS

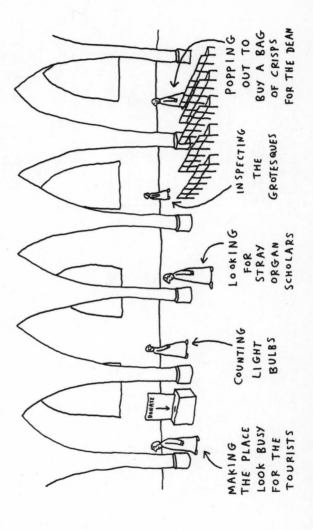

MAKING THE PLACE LOOK BUSY FOR THE TOURISTS

COUNTING LIGHT BULBS

LOOKING FOR STRAY ORGAN SCHOLARS

INSPECTING THE GROTESQUES

POPPING OUT TO BUY A BAG OF CRISPS FOR THE DEAN

THE CHAIR STRAIGHTENERS

YOU MAY HAVE SEEN THEM AT THE CATHEDRAL

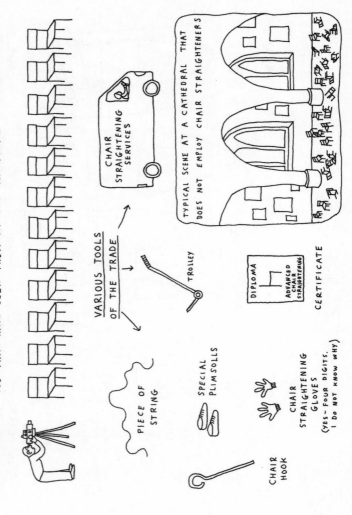

CHAIR STRAIGHTENING SERVICES

VARIOUS TOOLS OF THE TRADE

TROLLEY

PIECE OF STRING

SPECIAL PLIMSOLLS

CHAIR STRAIGHTENING GLOVES
(YES - FOUR DIGITS.
I DO NOT KNOW WHY)

CHAIR HOOK

DIPLOMA

ADVANCED CHAIR STRAIGHTENING

CERTIFICATE

TYPICAL SCENE AT A CATHEDRAL THAT DOES NOT EMPLOY CHAIR STRAIGHTENERS

PRESS OFFICERS

IT IS THEIR JOB TO MAKE THE CHURCH LOOK
SLIGHTLY BETTER THAN IT IS. THIS INVOLVES:

IS IT TRUE THAT HALF / WE PREFER TO
OF YOUR CHURCHES SAY THAT HALF
ARE FALLING DOWN? ARE STILL STANDING

DEALING WITH ENQURIES
FROM THE MEDIA

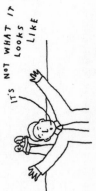

USING SCISSORS TO CUT INTERESTING
THINGS OUT OF THE NEWSPAPERS

TAKING PICTURES OF THE BISHOP
FROM THE MOST FLATTERING ANGLE

IT'S NOT WHAT IT
LOOKS
LIKE

TRYING TO MAKE SCANDALS LOOK
A BIT LESS SCANDALOUS

THE NATIONAL NEWSPAPERS

TRADITIONALLY THEIR GENERAL SYNOD REPORTS WERE COMPILED AS FOLLOWS:

 NOTES WERE MADE IN SHORTHAND

⇧ THEN THEY WERE WRITTEN OUT IN FULL

⇧  DICTATED VIA THE TELEPHONE

 ↳ TYPED UP BY A TYPIST

⇧  ENGRAVED ON TO STONE TABLETS

⇧  FINALLY, THEY PROVIDED INSPIRATION FOR A LITURGICAL DANCE COMPOSITION

THESE DAYS, THE RELIGION CORRESPONDENT, SITTING IN AN OFFICE SOMEWHERE, MAKES SOMETHING UP USING THINGS THAT FRIENDS HAVE POSTED ON TWITTER

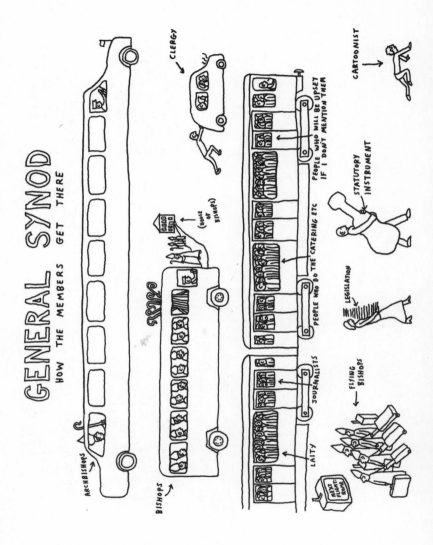

INVESTMENTS

WHERE THE CHURCH SHOULD PUT ITS MONEY

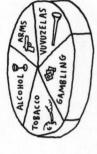

GOOD

IDEAS GIVEN AT THE CLERGY MEETING

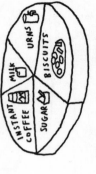

EVIL

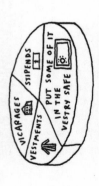

PORTFOLIO BASED UPON SUGGESTIONS RECEIVED AT THE COFFEE MORNING

THE CHURCH COMMISSIONERS

THEIR RESPONSIBILITIES

HOW WE HAVE _UNDERLINE_ INVESTED THE MONEY

GOOD

EVIL

BURIED IN A FIELD

MAINTAINING A BALANCED
PORTFOLIO OF ASSETS

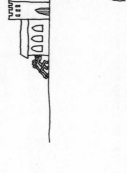

ESTATE AGENT

SPECULATING ON
PROPERTY

BROWN
ENVELOPES
TO BE POSTED

TAKING CARE OF BISHOPS'
PAY AND HOUSING

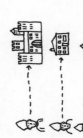

DISPOSING OF
UNWANTED CHURCHES

THE PROCUREMENT OFFICER

JOB DESCRIPTION: TO PURCHASE SUPPLIES IN BULK FOR THE NATION'S CHURCHES

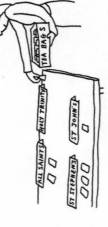

COUNTING OUT THE RATIONS

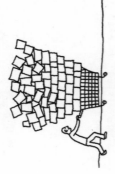

THIS INVOLVES DOING THE SHOPPING

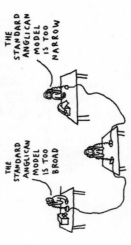

FIELDING THE INEVITABLE COMPLAINTS

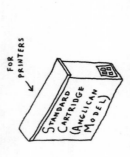

DECIDING UPON STANDARD MODELS

LENT

ACTIVITIES THAT ARE FROWNED UPON

EDUCATIONAL LEAFLETS

FREE SAMPLES

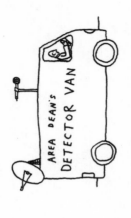

AREA DEAN'S DETECTOR VAN

PARISH BREWERY TRIPS

FOUL LANGUAGE ANYWHERE IN THE DEANERY

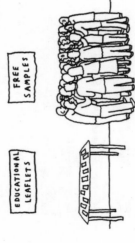

THIS AFTERNOON THERE IS A

BEETLE DRIVE

TICKETS VIA THE BOX OFFICE

HAVING TOO MUCH FUN

CHOCOLATE BISCUITS AFTER THE 10 A.M.

LENT

WOULD YOU LIKE TO JOIN OUR LENT COURSE?

IT IS KIND OF YOU TO OFFER, BUT NOT TODAY

CAN I INTEREST YOU IN OUR SPECIAL LENT WEBSITE?

NOT ON THIS OCCASION, THANK YOU

DO READ THIS LENT BOOK (WITH ASSOCIATED DISCUSSION QUESTIONS)

NOT THIS TIME, THANKS

PLEASE COME TO THE LENT LECTURES.

I WILL NOT BE ATTENDING, BUT THANK YOU FOR THE INVITATION

JOIN US FOR OUR LENTEN SERVICES

NO THANK YOU

HOW ABOUT A SPECIAL LEAFLET FULL OF DAILY LENTEN ACTIONS?

NORMALLY I WOULD, BUT TODAY I MUST REFUSE

LENT: A TIME OF ABSTINENCE

THE DATE OF EASTER

HOW IT IS CALCULATED

① THE 'DATE OF EASTER' COMMITTEE IS CONVENED

② SOMEONE POPS ALONG TO THE LIBRARY FOR A BOOK ON THE SUBJECT (AND TO CHECK SCHOOL HOLIDAY DATES ON THE INTERNET)

③ THE ARCHBISHOP HAS A LOOK THROUGH HIS TELESCOPE

④ THE HOUSE OF BISHOPS DISCUSS THE MATTER OVER LUNCH

⑤ THE PUBLIC ARE ASKED TO VOTE BY TELEPHONE

⑥ LETTERS CONTAINING THE RESULT ARE SENT TO CALENDAR COMPANIES THE QUEEN, ETC

THE PARISH CHRISTMAS TREE

THE THINGS THAT ARE HANGING ON IT (AND THE PEOPLE WHO HAVE DONE THE HANGING)

1 SPACE FOR LITTLE ANGEL, IF ANYONE CAN FIND ONE

2 CHILDREN'S INSTRUMENTS (NO ONE WILL ADMIT TO LOFTY PLACEMENT)

3 BELL (BELL RINGERS)

4 SAW USED TO CUT TREE DOWN (MEN'S GROUP)

5 TINSEL MADE FROM OLD SHREDDED SERMONS (THE VICAR)

6 BANNERS AND BADGES (UNIFORMED ORGANISATIONS)

7 TRADITIONAL NATIVITY ANIMALS — GOAT, ZEBRA, TRANSFORMER ETC (SUNDAY SCHOOL)

8 MEMORY STICK CONTAINING CHRISTMAS IMAGES (PARISH I.T. EXPERT)

9 TEA BAG (COFFEE ROTA VOLUNTEER)

10 CHURCH MOUSE (CHURCH CAT)

11 CORKS (SOCIAL COMMITTEE)

12 WRAPPED PRESENTS DESTINED TO FORM SLIGHTLY AWKWARD SERMON ILLUSTRATION

13 THURIBLE (HIGH CHURCH ENTHUSIAST)

14 HAND-KNITTED BAUBLES (LADIES' GROUP)

15 HYMN NUMBER CHAIN (SIDESPEOPLE)

16 DUSTERS (CLEANING VOLUNTEERS)

17 TRACT DISPLAY (LOW CHURCH ENTHUSIAST)

18 GLITTER (MESSY CHURCH)

19 ARGUMENT BETWEEN RIVAL 'COLOURED TREE LIGHT' AND 'WHITE TREE LIGHT' FACTIONS

20 BOX OF NON-COLOUR-SCHEME DECORATIONS REMOVED FROM TREE (BY UNNAMED PARTY)

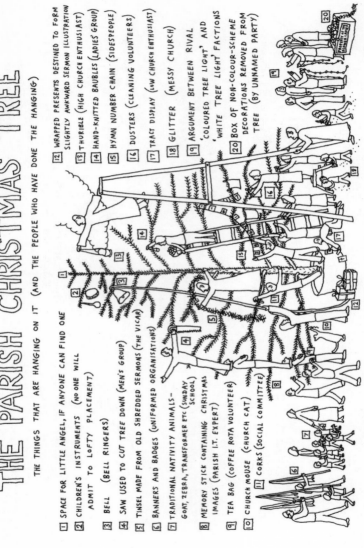

CHRISTMAS CARDS

THE FOOTBALL

IDEAS THAT COULD BE USED IN CHURCH SERVICES

THE SELLING OF
OVERPRICED PROGRAMMES

CHANGING DIRECTION AT HALF TIME

THE SHOWING OF SERVICES ON
BIG SCREENS IN THE PUB

YELLOW CARD
FOR MINOR
MISDEMEANOURS
(EG YAWNING)

RED CARD
FOR MAJOR
TRANSGRESSIONS
(EG MOBILE TELEPHONE
GOING OFF)

INNOVATIONS

THAT COULD CHANGE THE CHURCH AS WE KNOW IT

THE AUTOMATIC KNEELER

RISES UP TO CORRECT LEVEL FOR COMFORTABLE PRAYERS

THE HEAVY HYMNBOOK PULLEY

SERVES DOUBLE PURPOSE FOR CHARISMATICS

THE NOISELESS TOY

(SHAPE AND FUNCTION UNCERTAIN. DIAGRAM FOR ILLUSTRATIVE PURPOSES ONLY)

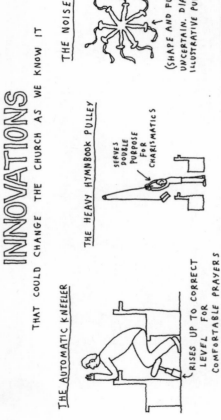

THE NEXT HYMN INDICATOR

NEXT HYMN NO 47

FLIPS AROUND LIKE TRAIN DEPARTURE BOARDS

THE ROTATABLE CONGREGATION

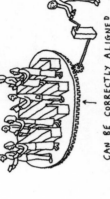

CAN BE CORRECTLY ALIGNED FOR GOSPEL, CREED ETC